THE CO ORGANIC BABY FOOD COOKBOOK

20 SPECIAL QUICK AND EASY ORGANIC RECIPES FOR BABIES AND TODDLERS

Dr. Samuel Jackson

Copyright (c) 2023 Dr. Samuel Jackson

TABLE OF CONTENTS

INTRODUCTION

ORGANIC BABY FOOD RECIPES

Recipe #1

Recipe #2

Recipe #3

Recipe #4

Recipe #5

Recipe #6

Recipe #7

Recipe #8

Recipe #9

Recipe #10

Recipe #11

Recipe #12

Recipe #13

Recipe #14

Recipe #15

Recipe #16

Recipe #17

Recipe #18

Recipe #19

Recipe #20

CONCLUSION

BONUS

7 DAYS MEAL PLAN

INTRODUCTION

Are you a loving parent who wants the very best for your precious little one? I understand that you want to provide the healthiest start in life, and that's why I am thrilled to write this organic recipes book for baby food.

Imagine feeding your baby meals made from the purest, organically grown ingredients. Say goodbye to harmful pesticides and additives that have no place in your baby's delicate system. With this organic baby food recipe book, you can nourish your baby with love and goodness, knowing that every bite is packed with essential nutrients.

The carefully crafted recipes in this book are designed to tantalize tiny taste buds and promote healthy development. It offers a variety of flavors and textures, allowing your little one to explore and enjoy a rainbow of culinary experiences. From sweet and savory purees to nutritious snacks, there's something to suit every stage of your baby's journey.

But it's not just about the delicious taste and wholesome ingredients. By choosing organic baby recipes, you're making a conscious decision to protect your baby's future. You're supporting sustainable farming practices that care for the environment and ensure a healthier planet for generations to come.

So why wait? Join the growing community of parents who are committed to providing the best nutrition for their little ones. Your baby deserves the purest, most nutritious meals, and I am here to help you make that happen.

ORGANIC BABY FOOD RECIPES

Recipe #1

BANANA OATMEAL PANCAKES

Ingredients

1 mashed ripe banana

Organic rolled oats in a half-cup

Organic whole wheat flour, 1/4 cup

1/2 cup organic milk (for infants, breast milk or formula)

A half-teaspoon of baking powder

Cinnamon spice, optional

Procedure

- ❖ Banana puree, rolled oats, whole wheat flour, milk, baking soda, and cinnamon (if used) should all be combined in a bowl. Mix thoroughly.
- ❖ With coconut oil or organic cooking spray, warm a non-stick pan over medium heat.
- ❖ When bubbles appear on the surface, drop spoonfuls of the pancake batter into the pan and cook.
- ❖ The pancakes should turn golden brown after another minute of cooking.
- ❖ Cut into toddler-friendly portions and serve warm.

- ❖ Make a larger batch and freeze the pancakes separately for meal preparation. For quick and simple breakfasts, defrost and reheat as necessary.

SWEET POTATO AND LENTIL PUREE

Ingredients

One small organic sweet potato, diced after being peeled

Organic red lentils, 1/4 cup

1 cup of organic vegetable broth or water

Procedure

- ❖ Sweet potato, lentils, and water or vegetable broth should all be combined in a small pot.
- ❖ Bring to a boil, then lower the heat and simmer for 15 to 20 minutes, or until the lentils and sweet potato are cooked through.
- ❖ Remove any extra liquid, then let it to cool a little.
- ❖ Use a blender or food processor to puree the ingredients until it is smooth.
- ❖ Serve hot or store in the fridge for later use.
- ❖ Tip for Meal Prep: Double the recipe and freeze it in ice cube trays in separate portions. When serving, defrost and reheat.

MINI VEGGIE FRITTATAS

Ingredients

Four organic eggs

4 ounces of organic milk

1/4 cup organic cheddar cheese, grated

Organic veggies (spinach, bell peppers, zucchini) in 1/4 cup finely chopped form

Pepper and salt as desired

Procedure

- ❖ Lightly grease a mini muffin tray and preheat the oven to 375°F (190°C).
- ❖ Eggs, milk, grated cheese, chopped veggies, salt, and pepper should all be combined in a bowl.
- ❖ Fill each cup in the muffin tin about 3/4 full with the mixture.
- ❖ The frittatas should bake for 12 to 15 minutes, or until set and gently brown.
- ❖ Serve them after they have cooled.
- ❖ Make a batch of small frittatas and keep them in the fridge for up to three days as a meal prep idea. Serve chilled or heated in the microwave as a quick snack or meal addition.

QUINOA AND VEGETABLE STIR-FRY

Ingredients

Organic quinoa boiled into a half-cup

A quarter cup of organic mixed vegetables (corn, peas, and carrots)

1 tablespoon low-sodium soy sauce or organic tamari

A single tablespoon of organic olive oil

Organic sesame oil, 1/2 teaspoon (optional)

Procedure

- ❖ In a skillet or wok, warm the olive oil over medium heat.
- ❖ When the mixed vegetables are soft, add them and stir-fry for a short while.
- ❖ Stir-fry the quinoa for an additional two to three minutes after adding it to the skillet.
- ❖ Give the quinoa and vegetables a drizzle of tamari sauce and sesame oil (if using). Mix thoroughly.
- ❖ Before serving, remove from the heat and allow it cool.
- ❖ Tip for meal preparation: Prepare the quinoa in advance and chop the vegetables. To make assembly and cooking when necessary easier, store them separately in the refrigerator.

Recipe #5

AVOCADO AND CHICKPEA SMASH

Ingredients

1 organic, ripe avocado

Mashed half a cup of organically grown chickpeas.

Fresh lemon juice squeezed

An optional pinch of organic cumin

Procedure

- ❖ Use a fork to thoroughly mash the ripe avocado in a bowl.
- ❖ Add the lemon juice, cumin (if using), and the mashed chickpeas. Mix thoroughly.
- ❖ Spread it on whole grain bread or use it as a dipping sauce for vegetable sticks.
- ❖ Make a bigger batch and keep it in the fridge for up to two days by storing it in an airtight container.

Recipe #6

MINI TURKEY MEATBALLS

Ingredients

Organic turkey ground up to half a pound

Organic whole wheat breadcrumbs in 1/4 cup

a single lightly beaten organic egg

1/4 cup organic zucchini, grated finely

A quarter-teaspoon of organic garlic powder

1/8 teaspoon dried organic oregano

Pepper and salt as desired

Procedure

- ❖ Bake at 375°F (190°C) for 15 minutes with a baking sheet lined with parchment paper.
- ❖ Ground turkey, breadcrumbs, egg, grated zucchini, garlic powder, dried oregano, salt, and pepper should all be combined in a bowl. Mix thoroughly.
- ❖ On the baking sheet that has been prepared, form the mixture into little meatballs.
- ❖ Bake for 15 to 20 minutes, or until thoroughly heated and lightly browned.
- ❖ Serve them after they have cooled.
- ❖ Make a batch of tiny turkey meatballs and freeze them separately as a meal preparation tip. For a meal alternative that is high in protein, thaw and reheat as needed.

Recipe #7

APPLE AND CINNAMON OATMEAL

Ingredients

Organic rolled oats in a half-cup

1 cup organic milk (for infants, breast milk or formula)

12 organic apple, chopped after peeling

1/8 tsp. organic cinnamon ground

1 teaspoon organic maple syrup or honey (optional)

Procedure

- ❖ Rolling oats, milk, apple dice, and cinnamon should all be combined in a small pot.
- ❖ To cook the oats and apple until they are soft, bring to a boil, then lower the heat and simmer for about 5-7 minutes.
- ❖ Take it off the fire and give it a minute to cool.
- ❖ If desired, sweeten with honey or maple syrup.
- ❖ Serve hot.
- ❖ Cook a bigger quantity and keep individual servings in the fridge for up to three days as a meal preparation tip. Before serving, reheat in the microwave or on the stovetop.

Recipe #8

LENTIL AND VEGETABLE SOUP

Ingredients

Organic red lentils, half a cup

Organic veggies (carrots, celery, and onions) in 1/4 cup finely chopped form

Two cups of natural vegetable broth

1/8 teaspoon dried organic thyme

1/8 teaspoon dried organic oregano

Pepper and salt as desired

Procedure

- ❖ Red lentils, diced veggies, vegetable broth, dried thyme, dried oregano, salt, and pepper are all combined in a pot.
- ❖ When the lentils and vegetables are cooked, simmer for 15 to 20 minutes after bringing to a boil.
- ❖ Before serving, let the soup somewhat cool.
- ❖ Advice for meal preparation: Double the recipe and freeze the individual servings in BPA-free containers for up to three months. When necessary, thaw and reheat on the stovetop or in the microwave.

Recipe #9

SPINACH AND CHEESE QUESADILLA

Ingredients

2 little tortillas made of organic whole wheat

Organic baby spinach greens, half a cup

1/4 cup organic cheddar cheese, grated

Cooking oil made with organic olives

Procedure

- ❖ A nonstick skillet should be heated to medium.
- ❖ Layer baby spinach leaves, shredded cheddar cheese, and one tortilla in the griddle.
- ❖ Place the second tortilla on top, pressing lightly.
- ❖ Cook the tortillas for 2-3 minutes on each side, or until they are golden brown and the cheese has melted.
- ❖ Slice it into little triangles after removing from the skillet and allowing it to cool somewhat.
- ❖ Tip for Meal Prep: Make a batch of quesadillas and store them in the fridge for up to two days. For an easy and enjoyable meal, reheat in a toaster oven or on a skillet.

Recipe #10

ROASTED VEGETABLE PASTA

Ingredients

1 cup organic whole wheat pasta, preferably in shapes that young children can handle.

1 cup of various organic vegetables, including cherry tomatoes, bell peppers, and zucchini

a single tablespoon of organic olive oil

1/8 teaspoon dried organic basil

1/8 tsp dried organic oregano

Organic Parmesan cheese, grated (optional)

Procedure

- ❖ A baking sheet should be lined with parchment paper and the oven should be preheated to 400°F (200°C).
- ❖ Olive oil, dried oregano, dried basil, and mixed veggies should be combined in a bowl.
- ❖ The vegetables should be spread out on the prepared baking sheet and roasted for 15 to 20 minutes, or until soft and just beginning to caramelize.
- ❖ Pasta should be cooked as directed on the package until it is al dente.
- ❖ After draining, combine the roasted vegetables with the pasta.
- ❖ If preferred, top with grated Parmesan cheese.
- ❖ Serve hot.
- ❖ A helpful tip for meal preparation is to roast more veggies than pasta and store them in the refrigerator separately. When you're ready to serve, combine them for a quick and filling meal.

Recipe #11

BLUEBERRY BANANA SMOOTHIE

Ingredients

Fresh or frozen organic blueberries equaling half a cup

1 banana, ripe and organic

Organic plain Greek yogurt, half a cup

1/2 cup organic milk (for infants, breast milk or formula)

1 tablespoon organic peanut butter or almond butter

Procedure

❖ Blend blueberries, banana, milk, Greek yogurt, and, if using, almond butter or peanut butter.
❖ Blend till creamy and smooth.
❖ Serve immediately after pouring into a cup or sippy cup.
❖ Tip for Meal Prep: Divide the blueberries and banana into freezer bags and prepare individual smoothie packs. When you're ready to serve, just combine the remaining ingredients after freezing them.

Recipe #12

CHICKEN AND VEGETABLE SKEWERS

Ingredients

1 organic chicken breast, diced into small pieces.

Cut into tiny pieces, 1/4 cup organic bell peppers

Sliced organic zucchini up to 1/4 cup

A single tablespoon of organic olive oil

Organic garlic powder, a pinch

A pinch of dried organic basil

A dash of pepper and salt

Procedure

- ❖ A baking sheet should be lined with parchment paper and the oven should be preheated to 400°F (200°C).
- ❖ Chicken cubes, bell peppers, and zucchini are threaded onto skewers.
- ❖ On the prepared baking sheet, arrange the skewers.
- ❖ Olive oil should be drizzled over the dish before adding salt, pepper, dried basil, and garlic powder.
- ❖ Bake for 15 to 20 minutes, or until the vegetables are soft and the chicken is thoroughly cooked.
- ❖ Before serving, let the skewers cool somewhat. Take the chicken and vegetables off the baby skewers.
- ❖ Meal Prep Tip: Make the skewers ahead of time and keep them chilled. When you're ready to serve them, grill or bake them for a tasty supper.

Recipe #13

BERRY CHIA PUDDING

Ingredients

A quarter cup of organic chia seeds

1 cup organic milk (for infants, breast milk or formula)

Strawberries, blueberries, and raspberries make up half a cup of organic mixed berries.

1 teaspoon organic maple syrup or honey (optional)

Procedure

- ❖ Chia seeds and milk should be mixed in a bowl. Stir thoroughly.
- ❖ To avoid clumping, give the mixture another toss after letting it sit for about 5 minutes.
- ❖ Overnight or for at least two hours, cover and chill.
- ❖ Stir the pudding before serving, then sprinkle the berries on top.
- ❖ If desired, sweeten with honey or maple syrup.
- ❖ Make a larger batch of chia pudding and keep it in the fridge for up to 4 days by storing it in individual containers. When you are ready to serve, add fresh berries.

Recipe #14

CAULIFLOWER MAC AND CHEESE

Ingredients

1 serving of organic whole wheat pasta

1 cup florets of organic cauliflower

Infant formula or breast milk, 1/4 cup organic milk

Organic cheddar cheese, 1/4 cup

1 tablespoon organic olive oil or butter

Organic garlic powder, a pinch

One organic nutmeg seed pinch

pepper and salt as desired

Procedure

- ❖ As directed on the package, prepare the macaroni until it is al dente.
- ❖ Steam the cauliflower florets until they are soft in a different pot.
- ❖ Transfer the cauliflower to a food processor or blender after it has been drained.
- ❖ Blender ingredients should include milk, grated cheddar cheese, butter or olive oil, garlic powder, nutmeg, salt, and pepper.
- ❖ Blend till creamy and smooth.
- ❖ Return the cooked macaroni to the saucepan after draining.
- ❖ Mix the macaroni with the cauliflower cheese sauce after pouring it over it.
- ❖ Heat gently until well warmed.
- ❖ Serve hot.
- ❖ Double the recipe and store any leftovers in the refrigerator in individual containers for up to three days. Reheat in the microwave or on the stovetop while stirring in a little milk to keep the dish creamy.

BROCCOLI AND CHEESE MINI MUFFINS

Ingredients

1 cup steamed and coarsely chopped organic broccoli florets

A single cup of organic whole wheat flour

Organic grated cheddar cheese, half a cup

1/2 cup organic milk (for infants, breast milk or formula)

A single lightly beaten organic egg

Organic olive oil, 1/4 cup

Organic baking powder, 1 teaspoon

A dash of pepper and salt

Procedure

- ❖ Prepare a tiny muffin tray with greasing and preheat the oven to 375°F (190°C).
- ❖ Chunks of broccoli, whole wheat flour, grated cheddar cheese, baking powder, salt, and pepper should all be combined in a bowl.
- ❖ Mix the milk, egg, and olive oil in a another bowl.
- ❖ Mix the dry ingredients just until mixed after adding the wet ingredients.
- ❖ Fill each cup in the prepared muffin tin about 3/4 full with the batter.

- ❖ A toothpick inserted in the center of the cake should come out clean after baking for 12 to 15 minutes.
- ❖ Before serving, let the mini muffins cool just a bit.
- ❖ Make a batch of small muffins and freeze them separately as a meal preparation tip. For a speedy and practical snack or dinner addition, defrost and reheat in the microwave or oven.

Recipe #16

TURKEY AND VEGETABLE MEATLOAF

Ingredients

Organic turkey ground up to half a pound.

1/4 cup organic vegetables (onions, zucchini, carrots) that have been finely chopped

organic whole wheat breadcrumbs in 1/4 cup

A single lightly beaten organic egg

2 tablespoons organic ketchup or tomato sauce

1/8 teaspoon dried organic thyme

1/8 teaspoon dried organic parsley

Pepper and salt as desired

Procedure

- ❖ Prepare a loaf pan with greasing and preheat the oven to 375°F (190°C).

- Ground turkey, finely chopped veggies, breadcrumbs, egg, tomato sauce or ketchup, dried thyme, dried parsley, salt, and pepper should all be combined in a bowl. Mix thoroughly.
- Place the mixture in the loaf pan that has been buttered, then press down firmly.
- The meatloaf should be golden brown and cooked through after 35 to 40 minutes in the oven.
- Slice it into parts that are suitable for toddlers after letting it cool for a few minutes.
- Meal prep tip: Make the meatloaf in advance and store it in the fridge or freezer before baking. Simply defrost (if frozen) and bake as directed when ready to serve.

Recipe #17

VEGGIE RICE BALLS

Ingredients

1 cup of organic brown rice, cooked

1/4 cup organic veggies (corn, peas, carrots) that have been coarsely chopped

2/fourths cup organic breadcrumbs

A single lightly beaten organic egg

Organic garlic powder, a pinch

A pinch of dried organic basil

A dash of pepper and salt

Cooking oil made with organic olives

Procedure

- ❖ Brown rice that has been cooked, chopped veggies, breadcrumbs, beaten eggs, dried basil, salt, and pepper are all combined in a bowl. Mix thoroughly.
- ❖ Form the mixture into little balls and firmly press down to help them maintain their shape.
- ❖ In a skillet over medium heat, warm the olive oil.
- ❖ The rice balls should be cooked in the skillet for three to four minutes on each side, or until golden and crispy.
- ❖ Before serving, take them out of the skillet and allow them to cool somewhat.
- ❖ Make a large batch of vegetarian rice balls and keep them in the fridge for up to three days as a meal preparation tip. Reheat in the oven or skillet for a wholesome addition to a snack or supper.

Recipe #18

APPLE CINNAMON BAKED OATMEAL CUPS

Ingredients

1 cup of rolled organic oats

Organic applesauce, half a cup

Infant formula or breast milk, 1/4 cup organic milk

A single lightly beaten organic egg

1 tablespoon organic maple syrup or honey

1/8 tsp. organic cinnamon ground

Organic vanilla extract, 1/4 teaspoon

A dash of salt

Procedure

- ❖ Paper liners should be used to line a muffin pan as the oven is preheated to 350°F (175°C).
- ❖ Rolling oats, applesauce, milk, beaten egg, honey or maple syrup, cinnamon, vanilla essence, and salt should all be combined in a bowl. Mix thoroughly.
- ❖ Fill each cup in the prepared muffin tray about 3/4 full with the oatmeal mixture.
- ❖ Bake for 20 to 25 minutes, or until golden brown and firm on top.
- ❖ Before serving, let the oatmeal cups to cool.
- ❖ Make a batch of baked oatmeal cups and store them in the refrigerator for up to 5 days as a meal prep idea. Reheat in the oven or microwave for a speedy and wholesome breakfast or snack.

Recipe #19

PUMPKIN AND CARROT SOUP

Ingredients

1 cup pureed organic pumpkin

A half-cup of organic, peeled, and sliced carrots

Two cups of natural vegetable broth

Organic coconut milk in 1/4 cup

A half-teaspoon of organic ginger

1/8 tsp. organic cinnamon ground

One organic nutmeg seed.

A dash of pepper and salt

Procedure

- ❖ Pumpkin puree, diced carrots, coconut milk, vegetable broth, nutmeg, cinnamon, ginger, and salt and pepper should all be combined in a pot.
- ❖ When the carrots are ready, simmer for 15 to 20 minutes after bringing to a boil.
- ❖ Take it off the fire and give it a minute to cool.
- ❖ Pour the soup into a blender or use an immersion blender to puree it.
- ❖ If necessary, reheat before serving.
- ❖ Make a larger quantity of the soup with the carrots and freeze it in individual servings in BPA-free containers for up to three months. When necessary, thaw and reheat on the stovetop or in the microwave.

QUINOA AND VEGETABLE STIR-FRY

Ingredients

Organic quinoa boiled into a half-cup

14 cup organic vegetables (carrots, bell peppers, and broccoli) that have been coarsely chopped

14 cup of frozen organic peas

A single lightly beaten organic egg

1 tablespoon organic tamari or soy sauce

A single tablespoon of organic olive oil

Organic garlic powder, a pinch

A dash of pepper and salt

Procedure

- ❖ In a skillet or wok, warm the olive oil over medium heat.
- ❖ Include frozen peas and diced veggies. Vegetables should be stir-fried for 3–4 minutes, or until they are soft.
- ❖ Pour the beaten egg into the space left by pushing the veggies to one side of the skillet.
- ❖ After the egg has cooked for a short while, scramble it using a spatula.
- ❖ Combine the vegetables and scrambled egg.

❖ Add the cooked quinoa along with the salt, pepper, garlic powder, soy sauce, or tamari. To fully reheat, stir-fry for an additional 2 to 3 minutes.

❖ Before serving, take it off the fire and let it cool somewhat.

❖ Tip for meal preparation: Prepare the quinoa in advance and chop the vegetables. For simple assembly and stir-frying when required, store them separately in the refrigerator.

CONCLUSION

In conclusion providing organic and wholesome meals for toddlers and babies is essential for their growth and development. These 20 recipes offer a variety of nutritious options to introduce new flavors and textures to young palates. By using organic ingredients, you can ensure that your little ones are consuming food free from harmful chemicals and pesticides.

Preparing meals for toddlers and babies doesn't have to be complicated or time-consuming. With proper meal planning and some meal prep tips, you can easily incorporate these recipes into your daily routine. Whether it's introducing new fruits and vegetables, incorporating whole grains, or adding lean proteins, these recipes are designed to provide balanced nutrition for your little ones.

By exposing children to a wide range of flavors and textures from an early age, you are laying the foundation for a healthy relationship with food. These recipes can be customized to suit your child's preferences and dietary needs. Don't be afraid to experiment and make adjustments as needed.

Remember to always prioritize food safety and hygiene when preparing meals for young children. Wash and prepare ingredients carefully, and follow proper cooking procedures to ensure that meals are safe and nutritious.

By investing time and effort in providing organic and nutritious meals, you are setting your toddlers and babies up for a lifetime of healthy eating habits. Enjoy the journey of introducing new foods to your little ones and watching them grow into healthy, happy eaters.

BONUS

7 DAYS MEAL PLAN

Day 1

Breakfast: Organic oatmeal cereal mixed with breast milk or formula.

Lunch: Mashed organic avocado.

Snack: Organic blueberry puree.

Dinner: Pureed organic sweet potato.

Before bed: Organic mashed banana

Day 2

Breakfast: Organic rice cereal mixed with breast milk or formula.

Lunch: Pureed organic butternut squash.

Snack: Organic applesauce.

Dinner: Mashed organic peas.

Before bed: Organic pureed mango.

Day 3

Breakfast: Organic barley cereal mixed with breast milk or formula.

Lunch: Pureed organic carrots.

Snack: Organic pear puree.

Dinner: Mashed organic green beans.

Before bed: Organic mashed papaya.

Day 4

Breakfast: Organic quinoa cereal mixed with breast milk or formula.

Lunch: Pureed organic broccoli.

Snack: Organic peach puree.

Dinner: Mashed organic zucchini.

Before bed: Organic pureed pineapple.

Day 5

Breakfast: Organic millet cereal mixed with breast milk or formula.

Lunch: Pureed organic spinach.

Snack: Organic plum puree.

Dinner: Mashed organic cauliflower.

Before bed: Organic mashed kiwi.

Day 6

Breakfast: Organic multigrain cereal mixed with breast milk or formula.

Lunch: Pureed organic green peas and carrots.

Snack: Organic strawberry puree.

Dinner: Mashed organic beets.

Before bed: Organic pureed papaya.

Day 7

Breakfast: Organic buckwheat cereal mixed with breast milk or formula.

Lunch: Pureed organic sweet potato and apple.

Snack: Organic apricot puree.

Dinner: Mashed organic squash and peas.

Before bed: Organic mashed banana and avocado.

Made in the USA
Columbia, SC
03 October 2023